HALF A TEAM

MICH

Tension runs hi
summer 5-a-side S
Rangers captain N
Dinger Bell, and
Sewell finds himse
superstars want re
the Festival and beat their old team-mates, they get together enough talent for a new team. But can the Swifts, trained and led by Nick, overcome all the obstacles before the Festival begins and will they really stand a chance of winning?

MICHAEL HARDCASTLE

Half a Team

Illustrated by Trevor Stubley

A Magnet Book

Also by Michael Hardcastle in Magnet Books:

IN THE NET

UNITED!

AWAY FROM HOME

FREE KICK

SOCCER SPECIAL

THE SATURDAY HORSE

First published in Great Britain 1980
by Methuen Children's Books Ltd
Magnet edition first published 1982
by Methuen Children's Books Ltd
11 New Fetter Lane, London EC4P 4EE

Reprinted 1984, 1987

Printed and bound in Great Britain by
Richard Clay Ltd, Bungay, Suffolk

ISBN 0 416 25210 9

One

Nick Abel-Smith raised himself on one elbow and stared bleakly at Dinger Bell. Dinger, arms folded tightly across his chest, glowed with exertion and anger. With the Great Summer Five-a-Side Festival coming up in a fortnight's time, tensions were running high. The other members of the Oakland Rangers squad cautiously drew closer in anticipation of yet another clash between their captain and vice-captain. This time, they sensed, it might actually erupt into physical violence. Inevitably, each of the players began to decide which of the two they would want to win if a fight took place. But even those who supported Nick doubted whether he had any chance of overcoming a much heavier and tougher opponent.

'Look,' said Dinger, speaking in a fairly low voice in a supreme effort to control his temper, 'this is crazy. This five-a-side lark only lasts ten minutes. So you've got to go flat out to bang in as many goals as you can in that time. There's no time to hang about and wait for the other side to make mistakes. We've just got to keep going forward and banging 'em in. Any other idea is as nutty as a fruit cake!'

That last phrase he delivered triumphantly. It was one he'd heard his uncle use frequently and effectively to clinch a point of view. Now Dinger had adopted it as his own. Usually, it drew an appreciative laugh from his audience; today, it raised only a couple of feeble grins.

'That's just typical of you, Dinger,' said Nick coldly. 'You never think there could be any alternative to your ideas – because you never *think*.'

Dinger took a sharp breath and stepped forward a pace. His audience tensed: they were sure he couldn't allow that insult to pass without striking a powerful blow in retaliation.

Instead, he suddenly swung round and lashed out with his right foot at the ball lying at the edge of their practice pitch. Involuntarily, everyone turned to watch its flight. It appeared inevitable that the ball, struck so fiercely, would soar over the goal area at the far end of the pitch. But then, much to the amazement of all of them, including the kicker, the ball dipped sharply and dropped into the net.

Dinger wasn't the type to miss a chance of exploiting one of his own feats, however unexpectedly it had been achieved.

'You see,' he crowed, 'that's just what I was talking about, Nick! If you keep banging away from all distances you're bound to score a few – especially when you hit 'em as well as that. If we followed your plan we'd have to dribble half the length of the pitch before anyone tried a shot. By then, somebody would have whipped the ball off your toe.'

He was well aware that his long-range goal, fluke though it was, had impressed a number of his team-mates. Trouble was, he couldn't be sure just how many of them were on his side. Very soon, though, he expected to find out.

Nick was now sitting up on the grass. Dinger judged that to be something in his own favour: he was *forcing* Nick Abel-Smith to take note of his skills as well as of his argument.

'That's *also* typical of you, Dinger,' Nick replied without raising his voice. 'You don't even know the rules of the game. You're just interested in brute force and the spectacular, however useless it is.'

'The rules!' Dinger roared. 'What's that supposed to mean? I know more about the rules than – than – than . . .'

'Right, then,' Nick said briskly, 'if you know so much, tell us why that shot of yours wouldn't have counted if this had been a five-a-side match played under competition rules. That's the way the Festival will be played, you know.'

'It *would* have counted,' Dinger insisted. 'It was a great shot. In fact, it ought to have counted double.'

'Rubbish,' said Nick, now getting to his feet. 'Even *you* know better than that, Dinger. Far from helping your side, that shot would have cost you a free kick, an indirect free kick. So by thumping the ball like that you would have *penalized* your own team.'

Dinger was seething. His instinct told him that Abel-Smith had somehow out-witted him yet again. But for the life of him he couldn't work out where he'd gone wrong. All he could do was pray that, for once, Abel-Smith had made a mistake.

It was Jazz Fagan who came up with the answer before anyone else.

'The ball was above head-height,' he pointed out. 'It would have whizzed high over my skull. And that's not allowed – I mean, to kick it over head-height, not just over MY head!'

'It may have been over Jazz's head but it wouldn't have been above *my* shoulder level,' Dinger declared, making the most of the fact that Jazz was one of the smallest players in the Sunday League.

'Oh, come off it, Dinger!' snapped Nick, at last displaying exasperation. 'You aren't the only player in the match, so the referee isn't going to measure everything by you. As Jazz says, the ball would have been above his head, so that's all that's necessary for the award of a free kick against your side. So they – we – would have been put at a disadvantage immediately.'

'Anyway, the ball would never have gone into the net,' remarked Jazz, encouraged by the response to his other comment. 'Their goalie would have saved it for sure. One-handed, probably.'

'Look, whose side are you on, Fagan? Let's be knowing,' Dinger demanded.

Jazz looked understandably surprised by that question. 'Why, ours, of course,' he said mildly. 'I mean, we are all playing for Oakland Rangers, aren't we?'

'I sometimes wonder,' mumured Jackie Allerton, the team's goalkeeper. 'I sometimes wonder,' he repeated, just in case someone hadn't heard him the first time.

Simultaneously, his captain and vice-captain wanted to know what he meant by that dark remark.

'Well,' said Jackie, who didn't often have the opportunity to express his views in the company of all his team-mates, 'I sometimes think that we're two teams, rather than one. I mean, you two are the cause of it. You never seem to agree about anything, do you? It's been the same ever since Nick won that Superstars contest and became captain. There's always a row about something and it's an absolute certainty that you two will be on opposite sides. Everyone knows that.'

Nobody tried to dispute it. For a moment or two, Jackie's words were followed by complete silence: it was almost as if he'd uttered an epitaph on the subject of their team. In a way, he had.

Nick was the first to defend himself. 'Well, as Jackie says, I am the captain. I won the *right* to make the decisions. It's my job to do that, to do what's best for the team. That's what a captain's for – to lead. I invited Dinger to be vice-captain because I thought he deserved some reward for finishing runner-up in the Superstars Contest. I also thought he would support me – I thought he would put Rangers first in everything. Instead –'

'I DO put Rangers first in everything!' Dinger cut in. 'I think of what's best for the team. That's what I'm trying to do now, so that we can go and win the Five-a-Side Festival. But, well, Nick is just going to make a mess of our chances if we play the way he wants us to. So –'

'See what I mean?' inquired Jackie of the other players. 'They're just getting to grips with each other, just like they always do.'

'Hang on, hang on,' Dinger appealed. 'Just let me finish what I wanted to say. Please.'

That quite astonished them. None of them could recall hearing Dinger Bell say 'please' for anything. It secured for him a fresh hearing.

'Look,' he went on, gratified by their obvious attention, 'I've always agreed that Nick is the captain, that he won the job fairly in the Superstars. But I think that planning the tactics of a team is a two-man job. Captain and vice-captain should decide between them what's best for the team. But Nick just runs things his way without – without *consulting* me. Or consulting anyone else.'

Dinger paused, almost as if expecting an interruption from Nick, but everyone simply waited for him to continue. They all knew that Dinger needed more than a dozen words to express his opinions. Nick was the one who summed things up concisely.

'Right,' Dinger resumed, 'you all agree that's the way it is, then. Well, I reckon that we've got to change our plans to fit in with what's needed for a five-a-side tournament. I believe we've got to go all out and attack from the word go. It's no use hanging back, waiting for a breakaway. Anyway, that's my opinion – and I think plenty of you agree with me. But Nick says the opposite, he says we've got to bide our time, soak up the opposition's attacks, then strike.

'I say that if we play Nick's way, we'll only play one match. We'll be knocked out of the competition almost before it's begun. Oakland Rangers will be finished.'

He stopped. For once in his life, Derek 'Dinger'

Bell, Rangers' dynamic, aggressive midfield ball-winner, knew the right moment to finish speaking to produce the best effect.

'I think Dinger's right, for once,' announced Jackie Allerton. That opinion was a shock to Nick, who had always considered the heavily-built but agile goalkeeper to be one of his supporters. Nick had never had a high regard for goalkeepers and if Jackie had turned against him he would think even less of them.

The rest of the team didn't say anything; they seemed to be waiting for their captain to state his case again, even though Nick had already told them what he wanted of them. Nick managed the most nonchalant of shrugs. He was at least twice as good a player as any of them: and he knew that they recognized that fact. They relied on him to show them how to play; they relied on him to work out the right tactics for a match. Dinger, as usual, had to take a different point of view for his own self-respect but when it came to playing he would accept Nick's authority. In every way that counted, the Rangers were Nick Abel-Smith's team.

'Think what you like, Jackie,' he said. 'Nobody takes any notice of your opinion. Goalies are just there to be shot at; they aren't capable of doing any shooting.'

The colour rose in Jackie's face but he didn't try

to retaliate. It wasn't a new experience for him to be insulted by his captain; Nick was scornful about everyone from time to time but he got away with it because of his own great talent both as a striker and as a ball-player. Even opponents who hated him admired his skills on the pitch. There wasn't another player in the Sunday League of his stature.

'Well, I tell you what I think,' said Dinger Bell, who suddenly realized that he'd been silent far too long. It was time the problem was resolved. It was time he took the lead.

'I think,' he went on, very slowly and very deliberately, 'it's time we won something. Won something big, I mean. With Nick as captain we haven't won anything. The best we've managed was sixth in the Sunday League. Well, nobody remembers who comes second, let alone sixth! We've played the way Nick wanted us to play – and that's done us no good at all. So I reckon it's time for a big change – a change to winning.'

He didn't have to wait long for support. 'I think Dinger's right – again!' said Jackie, and was delighted when a couple of the other players said, 'Hear, hear!'

Dinger was feeling bolder by the second. Now, he realized, was the moment to take the plunge.

'You going to stand down as skipper then, Nick?' he inquired.

'Don't be more stupid than usual,' was the cutting retort. 'You haven't a hope of winning without my leadership and tactical brain.'

By concentrating totally on what he had in mind, Dinger ignored that. 'O.K., lads, then it's got to be a vote. Who votes for me as captain – and a real chance of winning the five-a-side tournament?'

Immediately, five hands shot up, including Dinger's and Jackie's. Then, after the briefest hesitation, two more went up. Dinger was exhilarated: he'd done much better than he'd expected. With two of the Rangers squad absent from the meeting, he had won a vote of confidence by, at worst, seven-to-four. He couldn't resist the opportunity of twisting the knife.

'Who votes for Nick, then?' he chortled.

Jazz Fagan and Edward Lancaster, a red-haired midfield player, put up their hands. That left only one boy who hadn't voted (apart from Nick) and when Dinger demanded to know his view the reply was that he was still thinking about it. That, of course, didn't matter. Nick Abel-Smith had been overwhelmingly rejected by his team-mates at Oakland Rangers.

'That's it, then, Smithy,' said Dinger, knowing how Nick hated to be called that. 'All done very democratically. All very clear-cut. And you've been voted out of office. I'm in charge now and we're going to play my way in future.'

Nick swallowed hard and seemed to be on the point of speaking when Jackie Allerton, troubled now by the thought of his own treachery, asked:

'Er, Nick, you'll still be playing for us, won't you? I mean, the only difference is that Dinger is captain now.'

'Play for you lot after you've deposed me as captain?' Nick replied caustically. 'You must be as nutty as Dinger's fruit cake if you think I'd play for you again. I wouldn't play for Oakland Rangers even if you paid me.'

Dinger appeared delighted by that declaration but there was alarm on the faces of several of his team-mates.

'So what are you going to do, Nick?' one of them asked.

'Find a team that'll beat you lot hollow – and play for them,' was the answer.

Two

Two days later Nick Abel-Smith was on his way to a dog show. That wasn't at all where he'd expected to be on a summer Saturday but he supposed there were worse places. The most important thing as far as he was concerned was that Lester Rowan should have a successful and happy day showing his dog. Because, Nick believed, if all went well for Lester then he would probably agree to become the goalkeeper for Nick's new team that was to compete in the Five-a-Side Festival. In Nick's opinion, there were few better schoolboy goalkeepers around than Lester Rowan – when, that was, Lester concentrated exclusively on football and forgot for the duration of a match all about his pet animals.

In that dreadful moment when Nick had been replaced as captain of Oakland Rangers he hadn't really been thinking of what he would do next; he'd said he would find and play for another team simply because his pride wouldn't allow him to answer in any other way. Then, when he did wonder about his immediate future, he knew that nothing would give him more satisfaction than to do exactly that. He realized that, at this late stage of the proceedings, there was little chance of his being able to join an established team. All the competing sides would have to use their registered players, unless an emergency arose and they were permitted to take on new players. So his only hope was to form a completely new team. Provided he could get the players he wanted there would be no difficulty in entering the tournament: as the organizers were keen to encourage as many teams as possible to compete, the closing date for entries was still almost a week away.

Nick took comfort from two thoughts. One, that he had to find the equivalent of only half a team: five players were all he needed, and, if absolutely necessary, he'd be able to manage with four. Two, that if the players he had in mind turned out to be available then his team would be capable of winning *any* five-a-side contest in the county – probably, even in the country. From goalie to main striker (himself) they would possess all the skills needed to cope with any opposition. They would be a blend of tenacious defence and subtle, incisive attack. Above all, they would be ball-players.

Within an hour of the end of the meeting at which he'd lost the leadership of Oakland Rangers Nick had contacted two of his former team-mates at their homes. First, he had gone to see Edward Lancaster. He and Edward had first played together with Bank Vale United and later Nick had persuaded the carrot-haired wing-half to join him at Oakland Rangers. Edward had always been a strong, quick-thinking player; and, just as important in his captain's eyes, he had total respect for Nick's authority. If Nick's new five-a-side team was to win control in midfield and retain possession then it needed someone of Edward's calibre. Fortunately for Nick, Edward saw things that way, too, and had no objection at all to giving up his place in the Rangers team and throwing in his lot with Nick's as yet unformed squad. In any case, he and Dinger had been too similar in their style of play for Edward to feel that he would keep his place with the Rangers now that Dinger was in charge. It was predictable that Dinger would relegate him to substitute at the earliest opportunity.

There was no difficulty for Nick in recruiting his second player, either. Jazz Fagan was essentially fair-minded and he'd thoroughly disapproved of the way Nick had been treated by Dinger Bell and his cronies. His real name was James but because he'd started to sign himself Jas. Fagan (as his grandfather had done) he'd been nicknamed Jazz. In spite of his lack of height Jazz had a devastating burst of speed over a short distance and splendid control of the ball in tight situations. His strength was in his left foot and Nick felt that Jazz would complement his own skills as striker in a five-a-side game.

'Sure, Nick, I'd love to play for your team,' Jazz had said at once. 'Wouldn't it be great if we met Dinger's mob and thrashed them out of sight? With you and me playing together up-front we could score a net-full of goals!'

Nick had agreed that nothing would give him more pleasure. Not for the first time, he thought how much Jazz had changed in hardly more than a year. On first acquaintance, most people had the impression that the little left-winger was shy and lacking in any confidence at all. Yet he had entered the Superstars contest to find a new captain of Oakland Rangers and, after winning the 200-metre race and finishing second in the rifle-shooting event, he had held the lead for a time. After that success, followed by some fine displays of attacking wing-play in the very competitive Sunday Junior League, Jazz's real character had emerged; nowadays he could be assertive when he needed to be and he was usually ready to volunteer an opinion whatever the subject under discussion.

'What are you going to call your team?' Jazz had wanted to know.

'No idea,' replied Nick who hadn't given the matter a moment's thought.

'Well, I think a name's very important, Nick. Very important. Look, are there going to be any other players in it who can run as fast as you and me? You know, real speed merchants over a short distance?'

'Well, I hope so,' Nick admitted, 'but I can't tell yet. I haven't been able to see the other players I want to sign up. I mean, I came to you at the beginning – because you're going to be vital in our plans.'

If Jazz thought that was sheer flattery he wasn't unwise enough to say so. Instead, he eagerly explained what he had in mind. 'You see, Nick, I've always fancied the idea of playing for a team called The Swifts. Did you know that there are some American lizards called swifts? Swifts aren't only birds, you see. Anyway, these lizards can dart about like lightning – and that's how our team will play. We'll have to, won't we, to dazzle the opposition?'

'Er, well, maybe,' said Nick cautiously. He didn't want to dampen Jazz's enthusiasm but, equally, he didn't want to engage in tactical matters at this stage. 'Look, if that's the name you want us to use, well, it's O.K. by me. Actually, I quite like it. When the name goes on the draw sheet no one will know who we are. And that'll be a good thing. They're bound to worry about us just because we're an unknown quantity – a mystery team.'

Jazz was delighted that his suggestion had been taken up so – there was no other word for it – swiftly. He said so, adding, for good measure, that he was available to give any help that might be needed in organizing get-togethers and training sessions. It occurred to Nick at that point to offer Jazz the vice-captaincy of The Swifts; but, on reflection, he decided that honour ought to be kept in reserve, perhaps to be used as a bargaining factor when approaching one of the other players he was anxious to have on his side.

'Who else is going to be playing for us?' Jazz had inquired.

'Not absolutely sure yet because I don't know who's available,' confessed Nick. 'Just be my rotten luck to find that the guys I want are off on holiday during the Festival. But I'll let you know, Jazz, as soon as things are finalized. We'll all get together for training as soon as we can.'

'Make sure we have a good goalie,' was Jazz's parting comment. 'No good us scoring all those goals if some nut-case lets in dozens at the other end.'

That was precisely Nick's sentiment and the reason why he was about to attend his very first dog show. He and Lester Rowan had been members of the Town Boys' team which had made a close season tour and Nick hadn't forgotten the quality of some of Lester's saves. Unfortunately, Lester's interest in football had waned sharply in the wake of that tour. To the astonishment of the other players, he had taken with him his favourite guinea pig, a creature called Perkins; Lester had entered Perkins in a show at one of the towns they were visiting. Perkins had repaid his master's faith in him by winning first prize in his section. What few of his team-mates realized at the time was that Lester Rowan possessed something of a menagerie: in addition to guinea pigs he kept rabbits, two cats, a jackdaw with a broken wing, a mynah bird, dozens of fish in a variety of tanks, a tortoise and, so it was rumoured, a number of reptiles which had never been on public view.

Lester's latest acquisition, according to his mother, was a dog. Nick had heard about that when calling at Lester's home; Lester, though, was out, visiting a vet with whom, apparently, he was becoming very friendly.

'I've told him he's to be in by ten o'clock and I'll bet he's not here a minute sooner,' Nick was informed by Mrs Rowan. 'So I'm afraid you haven't a hope of seeing him tonight.'

'Perhaps tomorrow, then. . . .' Nick had ventured.

Mrs Rowan shook her head. 'No, that's no good. He's got jobs to do for me tomorrow and I'm not going to allow any distractions. There are enough of those around here as it is. Your best bet is on Friday when he's at the dog show. There's a lot of

waiting around for things to happen at those shows, so he'll be glad of somebody to talk to. Anyway, I expect you'll enjoy it. If you're a friend of Lester's you must be fond of animals.' Nick had no strong feelings in any direction about dogs but he wasn't going to admit that to Mrs Rowan: one day he might need her as an ally.

The show was being held in the Grand Hall in the town centre. Although it should have kicked-off, as Nick thought of it, almost an hour before he arrived, dogs of all kinds were still turning up in great numbers. He hadn't even guessed that so many varieties existed: Airedales and German Shepherds, Dobermanns and Dalmatians, Afghans and Old English Sheepdogs, pocket-sized Chihuahuas and mountainous Great Danes. Nick paid his entrance money and reflected that, when he became a club manager, it was the sort of outlay he'd be able to recover on expenses. To him, the smells and clamour in the main hall were fairly over-powering: but then, it seemed that he was just about the only person present who wasn't actually in charge of a dog.

Because he had no idea of the breed that Lester Rowan favoured at present, Nick had to make almost a complete circuit of the arena before he spotted his former team-mate. It had been split up, by the clever use of rows of seats, into four separate showing 'rings' and running down the

middle of each was a narrow strip of matting. It was along those strips that the entrants would parade and show off their paces.

Wearing what looked like a large rosette, but which bore a number and an advertisement for a pet food, on his shirt, Lester was leaning back contentedly in a seat by one of the outer rings. Sprawled on a blanket at his feet was a handsome, russet-coloured dog which Lester bent down to pat from time to time and whisper at in a manner which suggested he was encouraging it to do its best when the significant moment arrived.

'Hi,' said Nick, dropping into the seat next to Lester's. 'Are you all set to win a big prize today, then?'

'Nick – what are you doing here?' Lester had every reason to look astonished. It was months since he had seen the former skipper and chief striker of Oakland Rangers. 'I never knew you were keen on dogs. In fact, I seem to remember –'

'Oh, *everyone* likes dogs,' Nick put in hurriedly. 'I just dropped in, really, to give you a bit of support. I mean, I expect you'll be the winner, so it's a good thing to have a mate there to help you celebrate.'

By now Lester was thoroughly astounded. This was an aspect of Nick Abel-Smith he'd never imagined existed. Nick had something of a one-track mind: and that track led directly and only to association football. If people didn't share his interest, Nick had no time for them. Or so Lester had believed.

'But how did you know I was here? Today, at this time?'

'Oh, I have ways of finding things out I need to

know,' replied Nick loftily. He calculatedly lowered his hand towards the dog's head. 'All right to stroke your dog, is it? I mean, he doesn't *mind*, does he?'

'No, of course not! Atkins is very friendly and understanding. Sometimes –'

'*Atkins!* Isn't that what you called your, er, rabbit – the one you took on our football tour?'

'That was Perkins, and he was a guinea pig. And I know what you're going to ask next. Well, everybody seems to choose the same sort of name for dogs: Rover, Spot, Blackie, that sort of *ordinary* name. And I want something different. If you're going to show dogs, try to win prizes with them, then they've got to be obedient, they've got to respect you. You can't *command* a dog very easily by yelling Rover or Spot. But – Atkins! That really sounds good, doesn't it?'

The dog himself seemed to think so: he half-rose from his blanket, eyes moist with happiness, tongue lolling luxuriously. Lester fondled his best friend's head and ears; and Nick followed suit. The dog, whatever it was, seemed to approve of him.

'What, er, breed is he, then – Atkins?' Nick inquired, thankful he'd thought of the right word.

'Irish Setter – or Red Setter, most people call them. I think they're quite the best looking of all dogs, don't you?'

Because he had no firm opinion on the subject

Nick was able to agree with alacrity. So he said there was no comparison. Lester seemed very pleased with that response.

Around them there was a sudden flurry of activity. A small man with glossy black hair had moved into the centre of the ring; in one hand he had a sheaf of papers, in the other he was clutching a clipboard from which, in a booming voice, he began to read, very rapidly, a string of numbers.

Hastily, Lester got to his feet, bringing Atkins up with him as he did so. For a moment, he looked a little flustered.

'That's us, No. 167,' he said. 'I've been talking too much. I should have given Atkins a preliminary run-through, just to get his mind concentrated on what he has to do.'

'Oh, I shouldn't think that's necessary,' Nick remarked confidently. 'I'm sure you'll win easily.'

'I doubt it,' Lester said quietly. 'Atkins' record isn't exactly terrific yet. In fact, he's a maiden.'

Nick, not quite sure what that meant, watched with increasing interest as the competitors formed into a straight line on the far side of the strip of matting. Much to his surprise, he saw that not all the animals were Irish Setters; indeed, there were only three of that breed. The line-up included some amazing contrasts in sizes and shapes: miniature terriers and Pyrenean Mountain Dogs, poodles like geometrical puzzles and genuinely belligerent bulldogs. How on earth, Nick wondered, could a judge find points for comparison?

All the owners appeared to have equipped themselves with hairbrushes and, sometimes vigorously, sometimes tenderly, but always lovingly, were grooming their cherished charges. Occasional titbits were offered: but more often just shown than awarded. Legs were being rigidly moved into favoured positions, jaws were lifted, tails stretched out ... as, slowly, the glossy haired judge moved down the line. Not a smile was to be seen from judge or judged: the common facial expression was expressionless.

Nick tried to catch Lester's eye, but failed. Lester was, like every other owner, trying to appear unworried. When the judge moved in for a closer scrutiny on his second trip down the line Lester studiously avoided looking at the man. Then, as soon as the judge had gone on to the next, Lester shot an anxious glance at him. For Nick, it was impossible to guess what effect any of the dogs was having on anyone.

Eventually, the entrants were to be assessed on the way they walked: or, it appeared in most cases, ran. The judge stood at the end of the matting and, with an air of rather superior nonchalance, observed the manner in which tails wagged or flagged, hindquarters swayed or rolled, forepaws danced or slithered. To Nick's eye, Atkins had a splendid and elegant gait; but the judge's dour gaze gave nothing away.

Then, all the competitors lined up again for the judge's selection: quite rapidly now he indicated that four of them should step forward, over the matting 'wicket'; and the rest were waved forlornly away. Lester, with a still spirited Atkins ahead of him, rejoined Nick.

'Failed again,' Lester said gloomily, slumping into his seat. 'I'm beginning to despair of Atkins. He doesn't seem to know when we're being serious.'

'What's up with him?' Nick asked. He still thought Atkins was an excellent performer.

'Immature. Just needs more experience, I suppose. Can't see him winning any prizes for, oh, absolutely ages.'

Nick, with a striker's eye for an opening, recognized that the moment had come to pounce. 'But *you* could win a prize, Lester,' he said earnestly. 'Better than that – you could get a silver medal. A winner's medal.'

'What for?'

Nick outlined his plan for forming a team called The Swifts and entering it in the Festival. He explained that his first requirement was a top-quality fear-naught goalkeeper: and that was why he was asking Lester to join them. If, Nick concluded, he was able to field the side they wanted, then it would be the best in the tournament. Only sheer bad luck would prevent them from winning the Cup, the silver medals and the other prizes to be awarded to the winners.

He could tell that Lester was tempted; but the goalie remained silent, stroking Atkins' silky ears. Nick asked him what was up.

'I haven't played soccer for months,' Lester admitted in a soft voice. 'That's why you haven't seen me at Sunday League matches. I had to give it up. It was my Mum, you see. She said she wasn't prepared to go on looking after all the animals while I was off playing football. She had to do it when I was at school and it wasn't fair she should also have to do it when I was supposed to be at home.'

Lester paused. 'She was right, really. It wasn't fair on her. With my Dad being away from home so much, you see. She also said that if I got injured at soccer – broke an arm or something like that – well the animals would have to be got rid of, just like that. Funny thing was, the following week I did hurt my hand. Just a bad sprain. But it scared me. If anything happened to Atkins....'

Hastily, Nick steered his friend away from such depressing thoughts. Instead, he pointed out that the tournament would be taking place over a limited time – four half days at most, spread over a couple of weeks – and that it surely wouldn't be impossible to find someone willing to look after the animals during Lester's absence if his mother declined the job again.

'Yes, but who?' Lester inquired somewhat disbelievingly.

'Look, let's go and get some fresh air,' said Nick. 'I always think better on my feet. Atkins probably needs a run, anyway.'

Lester nodded his agreement and followed Nick up the wide staircase to a door that opened on to a sidestreet. Unerringly, Atkins made straight for the nearest lamp-post which, all too obviously, was already highly regarded by the rest of the canine population.

'Look,' Nick laughed, 'it's already starting to corrode! Honestly!'

And it was.

Some more competitors were coming along the street and Lester paused to run a trained eye over them.

'I think,' he told Nick in a serious tone, 'I'd like one of those next. It would be a good companion for Atkins.'

'What, a greyhound?'

'No. *That's* not a greyhound. It's a whippet. They're much smaller and –'

'Oh,' Nick grinned, 'I suppose that's because you want to grab the Whippet Cup!'

This time Lester joined in the laughter. He'd

never known Nick in such a jovial mood; indeed, he could hardly remember him cracking any jokes at all. Suddenly, he realized that he missed the comradeship of a football team, the fun in the dressing room when things were going well, the excitement of a big match. After all, he hadn't *wanted* to retire from the game. Quite by chance, Nick had touched on something that Lester thought about fairly often: he *would* like to win a medal of his own.

At the end of the street he automatically turned back to retrace his steps to the Grand Hall. Atkins was entered in two other events and very soon the next judge would be singing out competitors' numbers. This time, perhaps, Atkins might get one of the first four places.

Lester made up his mind.

'Are you sure you'll be able to get somebody to look after my animals if I play in goal for you?' he asked Nick.

'Oh, sure,' replied Nick, who was sure of nothing of the sort. Still, he'd think of something when the time came.

'Right, then,' said Lester emphatically. 'I'll play. I'll start training tonight.'

'Great!' Nick enthused. 'You won't regret it, Lester. We're going to win that Cup between us.'

Three

While Nick was suffering the humiliation of being ousted by Dinger Bell, Steve Sewell was wondering bitterly how much longer he would be captain of The Panthers.

He slammed the door behind him and then turned and aimed a kick at it. The only reason he didn't deliver the kick was his fear that he'd injure his foot; and an injury of that sort might really finish off his chances of playing in the Five-a-Side Festival.

Rather to his surprise, neither of his parents pursued him from the sitting-room. His noisy departure was apparently going to remain unchallenged. To Steve, that was a fair indication that at least his father sympathized with his feeling about having to spend almost a whole week in Manchester. All the same, that didn't mean that there was a chance of a reprieve for Steve. Yet again his mother would insist that he was still too young to stay at home on his own. His parents didn't have rows with each other, so, doubtless, his father would agree with her – yet again.

Steve didn't doubt, either, that there *would* be a row when he told the rest of the lads that he might not be able to play in any of the matches in the early stages of the tournament. He guessed that some of them would say that if he didn't turn out for the side in the first matches then he shouldn't be allowed to return for the final rounds of the competition: assuming, of course, that The Panthers progressed so far. Tommy Kent would certainly be one player who'd take that view. But then, Tommy wanted to run the team, anyway, and he would seize on Steve's absence to take it over completely.

As he left the house and set off for the Signal Box, where the squad met to discuss all relevant soccer matters, Steve Sewell chewed on the inside of his lip. A week ago he hadn't a care in the world. Now he was beset by all manner of problems.

His route led him across the corner of Lowbell Lane Sports Ground where the Five-a-Side Festival would be taking place in a fortnight's time. To Steve, it represented a wonderful chance to prove to his old team-mates with Merrywood Colts just how wrong they'd been to drop him from their side. For days he had been dreaming of little else but a Festival Final in which he skippered his team, The Panthers, to a scintillating victory over the Colts. Just to add an even sharper edge to his imagination, he included a sequence in which he himself scored a hat-trick in the last minute of the game.

Steve had played for Merrywood Colts for most of the previous season in the Sunday League. Although he'd been operating as an out-and-out winger he'd scored four goals, three of them from solo runs, and he was justifiably proud of that achievement. Yet, when the season was over and details were announced of the forthcoming Festival, his name was missing from the list of seven players from whom the Colts would choose their side. Naturally, he had tackled the captain about it immediately, but had met with an absolute refusal to reconsider the make-up of the squad.

'Sorry, Stevie, but you're just not good enough,' the captain had said in his customary blunt manner. 'You can move a bit, yes, I'll give you that. But you just don't have enough skills on the ball.' He paused and then added, as if quoting from a handbook: 'The fewer players there are in a team, the more skilful those players have got to be.'

Steve had protested that he'd been skilful enough to score those four goals; that he was the *fastest* player the Colts had ever had (which was absolutely true); and that he'd contributed a good deal to the team's tactical planning. The captain, though, wouldn't relent: and his decision was final.

So Steve, determined to take part in the Festival, had set about the task of finding enough suitable players to form an entirely new team. Fortunately, there was no restriction on the number of entries, so long as they were in the hands of the organizers by a certain date, and there were plenty of other boys who had also been rejected for one reason or another by their original teams. All the same, it hadn't been easy to find *quality* players who would blend together into an efficient unit under his leadership. Several were so bitterly resentful of the treatment they'd received from their former teams that they were in no mood at all to accept orders or advice from a new captain. For some days he'd despaired of getting a goalkeeper – any goalkeeper – but eventually he and Tommy Kent had tracked one down almost on the other side of the town. Their goalie's name was Mark Varley and there was no doubt that *he* was a player of considerable ability; unhappily, he was also injury-prone. Still, as Steve pointed out, goalkeepers were much less vulnerable in five-a-side soccer.

Tommy was Steve's first ally – and his first problem. Tommy prided himself on being 'a hard man': he played hard, he tackled ferociously at times and he could take any number of knocks without flinching. But his aggression, allied to his temper, had led him into numerous trouble spots from which, as often as not, he had emerged with a severe warning or with a definite 'booking'. He had been sent off more times than any other player in the Sunday League. His former team weren't prepared to risk that happening in a five-a-side match.

Tommy himself believed that if he were given more authority and responsibility during matches it would help him to control his temper; or, at least, that was what he said when Steve asked him to join his team for the tournament. He was keen to share the captaincy but Steve wouldn't concede that; after all, it was *his* team. Instead, he suggested that Tommy should act as co-selector. And with that Tommy had to be content. 'For the moment,' Tommy had muttered to himself under his breath at the time.

At a rather slower pace now, Steve continued on his way to the team's meeting place, an abandoned signal box. The old railway track through a fairly deep cutting had been taken up long ago; grass had grown where the sleepers lay and although the surface was uneven in places the whole area, enclosed by high banks, was splendid for football training sessions.

Steve climbed the by now fairly rickety outside

staircase that led to the only door into the box. Rather as he'd expected, Tommy Kent had arrived ahead of him and was seated on the wooden crate that was normally used by the player appointed as look-out, who would stand on it to scan the approaches to the signal box.

'You're late,' said Tommy briskly as soon as his captain entered the room. 'And so are the rest of 'em. The discipline's pretty hopeless in this team already, in my opinion.'

'I'm lucky to be here at all. In fact, half-an-hour ago I thought I might never be playing football for the team again – ever.'

As soon as he'd admitted that, Steve wished he hadn't. Tommy would always pounce on any weakness, as he did now, by demanding that Steve explain exactly what he meant. Steve hesitated, unwilling to confess everything. He'd had a faint hope that he just might gain Tommy's sympathy. He should have known better.

'Come on,' Tommy urged. 'I'm entitled to know everything. Remember, I'm deputy captain as well as co-selector.'

Before Steve could begin his explanation, however, there was a clatter of footsteps on the staircase and, next moment, three other members of the team burst in. Tommy was the first to greet them and he added:

'Steve, here, was just going to tell us something

important – about how he was going to give up playing for The Panthers.'

'I didn't say that!' Steve protested. 'I was talking about being *prevented* from playing. By my parents – well, my mother, actually. I wouldn't stop for any other reason.'

'Get to the point,' said Tommy.

Steve cleared his throat. 'Well, you see, it's my grandmother. The one who lives in Manchester – my father's mother, actually. Normally we just go and visit her twice a year, but only for weekends. But now my mother wants us all to go for a week – a *whole* week. Just when –'

'I thought you said your grandmother was your father's mother,' observed Mark Varley, who always paid attention to small details.

'She is, but my mother gets on better with Gran than my Dad does. Funny, I know, but that's how it is. My Mum says we don't spend enough time there and my Dad seems to have given in to her. The terrible thing is, the visit clashes with the first two dates for the Festival matches. There's just no way I could get back from Manchester for those. It takes more than half-a-day to get there on the train, the way we go.'

'Does your grandmother like football?' Robert Hopton asked innocently.

'No, she hates it! She says it's a stupid, violent game in which everyone gets injured sooner or later. She says some players just go looking for trouble on the pitch. She –'

'She wouldn't approve of you, then, would she, Tommy?' Mark grinned.

Tommy beamed at that comment. He liked his team-mates to appreciate his talents in sorting out the opposition. He realized, too, that, if it came to a vote on team matters, he'd most likely be able to count on Mark's support. At present he wasn't quite sure about Bobby Hoppy, as Robert was often called.

'Well, couldn't you stay at home on your own?' Robert persisted. 'I mean, you could look after yourself, couldn't you, Steve? Get your own meals and that sort of thing.'

Steve shook his head slowly. ''Fraid not. My mum wouldn't hear of it, she said. I suppose it might have been different if we'd had any relatives living near here but we haven't. . . .'

'Well, you could stay with someone else, then,' Robert went on, refusing to give in. He'd never said so, but he was grateful to Steve for giving him the chance to play in the Festival.

'You couldn't stay with us because we haven't any spare room,' Tommy put in quickly before that idea could be explored.

'We haven't, either,' Mark added with equal speed.

There was no need for Robert to explain his

position. All the boys knew that he and his mother lived on their own in a tiny flat and she didn't encourage any visitors at all.

Steve sighed deeply. None of them seemed to understand that he simply couldn't avoid going to Manchester. He supposed he hadn't made that clear enough to them. The thing he needed to know from them was whether they'd allow him to remain a member of the squad after missing the first few matches of the tournament. By this stage of the discussion he'd hoped to have won their sympathy for his plight; but, judging by the attitudes of Tommy and Mark, there was no sympathy at all on offer in that quarter. Still, he had to find out what they'd say. So he asked.

'Impossible!' Tommy stated at once. 'I mean, it just wouldn't be fair, would it?' he appealed to the other pair. But he didn't wait for any response. 'If we do get through the first few rounds it just wouldn't be right to drop someone who'd played in all the matches to make way for you. You can't run a team like that. It'd upset our tactical planning, anyway.'

Mark was nodding his agreement. Bobby Hoppy just looked blank. He'd already guessed that Tommy would take over the team and he didn't want to risk falling out with the new captain. All the same, he felt very, very sorry for Steve who'd done so much to build up the team.

Then, just as Steve was about to ask Robert for his views, the missing players turned up. Before either of them could say a word, Tommy Kent was on his feet and addressing them.

'Steve's just told us that he's got to go to Manchester and can't play in the Festival, so we've got to get somebody to take his place,' he announced decisively. 'It's rotten luck on Steve but the team's got to come first. As co-selector, I'll have to take over as captain and organizer. Nobody objects to that, do they?'

The two newcomers looked a trifle stunned. But they nodded their heads. With Tommy in such a commanding mood, they felt they could hardly do otherwise.

'Right,' said Tommy. 'That's settled. As it happens, I've a good idea who we could get to play up front. In fact, I think I ought to go and see him today and tell him what I want him to do for us. You can come with me, Mark, as co-selector.'

In that way, and with such speed, Steve's fate was decided.

Four

Tommy Kent was screaming for support: and getting none at all. Robert Hopton had taken a knock on the knee and was thinking only about avoiding the risk of any more pain. Only Mark Varley in goal showed any semblance of calm. So far the ball hadn't been put past him into the net and therefore he had little to worry about. Nonetheless, he rarely took his eye off Steve Sewell, who was playing some inspired stuff. Mark admitted to himself that he'd been rather lucky to keep out two of Steve's shots: one from close range that he'd deflected with his knee, the other fired in unexpectedly on the turn and accurate enough to clip the upright. Yes, Mark decided, it was a pity Steve wouldn't be playing for The Panthers in the Festival.

Steve himself had been thinking exactly the same ever since he'd been deposed as captain by Tommy Kent at the meeting in the Signal Box. That had been a great blow to his pride as well as to his ambition but it hadn't deterred him from trying to help the Panthers to build a winning team. He still wanted them to succeed, even though he was no longer going to be a playing member of the side. So, when practice sessions were arranged, he was eager to take part; and, not least because they needed all the players they could find on these occasions, the rest of the squad welcomed his presence. Of course, Tommy made it plain from the outset that he was the captain, that he was in *sole* charge, but by now Steve had accepted the loss of authority. Curiously, he found that he was playing better than at any time in his life. His ball control, passing and timing had all suddenly improved. Even his speed seemed to have increased.

It did occur to him at one point that he might have become a better player as a result of being relieved of the captaincy. But then he dismissed that idea. After all, he had really *enjoyed* leading the Panthers into action and making sure that each of his team-mates was playing to the best of his ability.

For the moment, however, Steve was getting a lot of fun out of opposing The Panthers. By playing as hard as he knew how for The Rest (a team made up of official reserves and anyone else who was keen to have a game) he was helping to locate any weaknesses The Panthers possessed. Then something could be done about them before they took part in their first Festival match. Tommy had said he'd be very grateful for that kind of support from Steve: it would be really constructive.

Actually, Tommy wasn't feeling very appreciative at present: for it was Steve himself who was giving him the run-around. Tommy had been trying hard to rid himself of his 'iron man' tag because he, too, recognized the problems the Panthers would be faced with if he were to be sent-off again in a Festival game. Discipline was what he was aiming to bring to his play: tackling forcefully but always fairly. And, somehow, that wasn't working at all. Steve, for one, was getting past him all the time, dummying and swerving his way through the defence with horrifying ease. Once – infuriatingly – he'd even nutmegged him: slipping the ball between Tommy's ankles and then nipping round him to collect it again. Nobody had ever got away with that trick before where Tommy was concerned.

'You're not shaping at all, Bobby!' Tommy screamed at Robert Hopton. 'Get stuck in! Get that ball off 'em! Fight for everything.'

Bobby was beginning to annoy him. He was sure the lad was a softie. Bobby had complained about a knee injury but Tommy could see nothing wrong with the leg. It was an excuse for the way Steve Sewell was out-smarting him.

Bobby shot him a look of pure hatred. 'Anybody else'd give up completely if they'd been hurt like I have,' he retaliated. 'I'm only staying on the field for nuisance value.' That was a phrase he'd heard a radio commentator use and now he'd adopted it as his own.

'Rubbish!' Tommy told him curtly. 'Get stuck in. There's only about a minute to go to half-time. You can have a rub down then.'

He didn't suggest who was going to do the rubbing down but he had himself in mind if necessary. He'd soon put some life back into the malingering Hopton.

Steve, collecting the ball from a throw-in, retained possession by rolling the ball under the sole of his boot and then backing-off. He knew that sooner or later Tommy Kent would have to rush him. Tommy, glowering with exertion and determination, advanced slowly – and then, without warning, leapt in with both feet. Steve, anticipating just such a move, spun away as his opponent took off and then, very neatly, flicked the ball on with the outside of his right boot to his co-striker, Simon Pink.

'A one-two, Simon!' Steve instructed.

Simon duly obliged after taking the ball right up to Bobby Hopton; and then as Bobby edged towards him, laying it off with commendable speed.

Steve took the ball in his stride, saw that Mark Varley was right on the perimeter of his area (and dithering) and, with minimum effort, slid the ball past the goalkeeper and right into the middle of the net.

He wheeled away and went to congratulate Simon Pink.

'Great ball, Rosey, great ball! Tommy ought to have you in the side.'

Simon's smile was rather lop-sided. He was pleased to be praised but he detested being addressed as Rosey, so much so that if Steve had used that name when calling for the pass he wouldn't have received it. Which Steve understood perfectly: but he couldn't resist employing the nickname from time to time. For one thing, Simon, a rather chubby youth, often had a rosey-pink complexion.

The goal was a most satisfying triumph. It was Steve's second of the match and now The Rest were leading The Panthers by a margin of 3–1. What's more, the first team's goal had only been scored from the penalty spot. The award of the penalty was dubious in Steve's opinion. One of his defenders *may* have put a foot inside the goal area; and that alleged infringement had caused Tommy to insist on a penalty kick. To shut him up, and because it didn't matter really one way or the other, Steve had agreed to concede it. Tommy himself had taken the kick and scored with a fierce and well-aimed shot.

As the successful strikers trotted back to the centre circle Tommy signalled that it was half-time. He had had enough for the time being. Accordingly, the two teams went into tactical huddles out of earshot of one another.

The match was being played on The Panthers' favourite pitch in the railway cutting near the old Signal Box. Because it lay on a favourite route for strollers and courting couples one or two passers-by had paused to watch for a few minutes. Now, however, the remaining spectators, with no action to enjoy, resumed their strolls. With the exception, that is, of one rather thin-faced, dark-eyed boy of about the players' age: Nick Abel-Smith. He had come upon the match by chance as he took a short cut; and, as he had time to spare, he'd stayed to watch.

Sitting on the steps of the Signal Box, he had virtually a grandstand view. At first, he'd supposed it was just a kick-about; but then, having noted the deadly seriousness of some of the play, he realized that at least one of the teams must have the Five-a-Side Festival in mind. Having clashed with him on more than one occasion in the Sunday League (and, indeed, been sent off in his company for retaliation), he'd instantly recognized Tommy Kent. What rather surprised him was that Tommy was skippering the side: Nick had never regarded the fiery Kent as the leader type.

Most of the other players were unfamiliar to him and, in his opinion, didn't amount to much where real skill on the ball was concerned. One of the two exceptions, though, was the tall-ish, blond-haired boy who'd been giving Tommy such a bad time. It was a while before Nick remembered which Sunday League team he played for: then it came to him, Steve something-or-other of Merrywood Colts. Steve Sewell: that was it! Well, Sewell had certainly come on a bit in recent months from what Nick remembered of his play. What puzzled him was why Sewell should be playing for this outfit: on the form he was displaying he was a certainty for the Colts' chosen five. One burst of acceleration on the ball had been positively electrifying. In Nick's rapidly calculating brain, it had set wheels in motion.

Meanwhile, Steve himself was summing up his ideas on how his team should play in the second half to hold on to their two-goal lead.

'You know Tommy'll start coming forward to get a goal himself. Bound to. Well, that'll give us the opening we want. Then, another breakaway – and bang! We're three up. Bobby Hoppy looks really all in. I think he *has* damaged is knee. So, we just play it around until Tommy gets desperate – and that'll be it.'

No one disputed it. None of them was taking the game as seriously as Steve. They knew that, unless their luck changed dramatically, they were just there to make the numbers up. Tommy had already picked his first team. The outcome of this practice match meant nothing to them.

It meant something to Tommy Kent and he was still dinning into his players what he expected of them.

'You've seen for yourself that Steve Sewell is just trying to take the micky out of us, me especially. It's natural, I suppose, but I'm not standing for it. I wouldn't stand for it in a League match or a Festival match. So he's got to be stopped. O.K.?' He waited for a response but none was forthcoming. The Panthers were getting just a shade fed up of their captain's constant hectoring. After all, he wasn't performing so brilliantly himself.

'It's up to you, Bobby, to stop him,' Tommy ordered when he resumed. 'You've got to put him out of the game. O.K.?'

'Why me?' Bobby protested. 'You know my knee is – '

'Oh, stop wailing, Hopton! You know I can't do it. I've got to practise keeping me temper. So I can't go and clobber him now.'

'You'd probably not be able to catch him the way Steve's playing,' Mark Varley murmured, in just too low a tone for Tommy to hear it. In a louder voice he added: 'I think Rosey's playing pretty well. He's a danger man, too, Tommy. Stevie's playing off him, you know. All those one-twos. Very effective.'

Tommy wasn't prepared to consider other problems at present. 'Come on, let's get on with it. Let's take 'em apart this time.'

So the second half began in precisely the fashion that Steve had predicted. The only thing that surprised him was that Bobby Hoppy seemed to have recovered from his ailment. Every time Steve had the ball, Bobby was chivvying him and trying to knock him over.

'Ease off, Hoppy, or I'll smash your other knee next time,' Steve warned mildly. He had no such intention. He thought the threat would be enough to keep Bobby off his back. But to emphasize the point he gave him a gentle push.

Next moment Tommy cannoned into him with crushing force. As Steve stumbled, The Panthers' captain caught him in the face with his knee. Steve went down flat and stayed there.

'If you assault one of my team, you assault me!' Tommy yelled at him. His fury was all the greater because his team still hadn't pulled a goal back.

Nick, still sitting on the Signal Box steps, began to clap ironically. Tommy was running absolutely to form. There wasn't much doubt that his team would be under a lot of extra pressure in the Festival matches.

Until that moment, Tommy hadn't been aware of Nick's presence. But he recognized the solitary spectator immediately. Moving as fast as he'd done all day, he raced across to the Box.

'I don't know what the hell you think you're doing here, Smithy,' he yelled, 'but you're not wanted. You're spying on my team! Well, you can get lost! Right now.'

Nick scowled. As ever, the 'Smithy' bit was the worst insult of all. One of these days he was going to get even with Tommy Kent. But today wasn't that day. He had other, much more important, matters to attend to and so he wasn't going to waste time and energy on a lout like Tommy Kent.

'You're not worth watching,' Nick retorted, moving down the steps as nonchalantly as possible. 'There's no point in spying on what *you* call a team. You're just vandals on a soccer pitch!'

Pleased with that description, he sauntered away along the cutting. Tommy Kent's inclination was to rush after him and flatten him for good. But then, at last, he remembered that he was trying to harness his temper. He was becoming aware, too, that his team-mates were eyeing him with trepidation after his violent treatment of Steve Sewell. If

their new captain could do that to one of their own side. . . .

But Steve pushed him away when Tommy tried to apologize. 'Leave off, Kent! I've had all I can take of you. You're just a – a thug! Well, you're not going to have me to knock around any more.'

Tommy, as usual, was eager to defend his conduct but Steve meant what he said: he was in no mood to listen. The right side of his face was still aching with the force of the blow he'd taken. He didn't want any false sympathy: he just wanted to get out of the sight of all of them. He'd be thoroughly happy if he never saw any of The Panthers again. Steve was finished with them.

Grabbing his track-suit top, he ran.

Nick, still strolling along and contemplating a mental list of possibilities for the composition of his own team, The Swifts, turned and then waited when he heard Steve behind him. Earlier in the day he'd received a setback to his plans: the player he'd been hoping to sign up as forward was going to be abroad on holiday during the festival. It was infuriating but nothing could be done about it.

So, for the present, The Swifts were short of at least one player. Ideally, Nick would have liked a squad of seven; even six players, with one of them on hand as a possible substitute, would provide him with some sense of well-being. In reality, he probably was going to have to settle for the basic five.

Himself, Lester Rowan, Jazz Fagan, Edward Lancaster, and . . .

'How're you feeling now, Steve?' he inquired with plenty of warmth in his voice. 'It's time that maniac Kent was banned from all soccer matches. One of these days he's going to kill somebody.'

Steve appreciated the sympathy he was getting; but, more than that, he was flattered that Nick Abel-Smith had remembered his name and waited to talk to him. After all, Nick was one of the real stars of the Sunday Junior League and it was well known that a professional club was keeping an eye on his progress. Now, just as if they'd been friends for years, they fell into an easy conversation as they walked along side-by-side and soon Steve was explaining what had happened with Merrywood Colts and how Tommy Kent had cheated him out of the leadership of The Panthers.

'I thought you played some great stuff today – you personally, I mean, not the rest of that bunch,' Nick told him. 'You showed terrific speed at times. I was very impressed, Steve.'

'Er, oh, thanks, Nick.' Steve had never been praised like this by a fellow player. He didn't know what to say.

'Yeah, never seen you play better,' Nick was going on. 'I was thinking, we could do with your speed in my team. Especially after the way you were controlling the ball and shooting right on target. Could be a winning combination, you and me up-front.'

Steve, of course, thought he was referring to Oakland Rangers. Then, when he learned that he was being invited to join a team that Nick himself had formed, he was even more delighted. Any player in the Sunday Junior League would regard that as an honour. On top of everything, it would give him a tremendous chance of getting his own back on Tommy Kent and his ex-team-mates (from both The Panthers and from Merrywood Colts). A team led by Nick Abel-Smith was bound to be full of quality and initiative and was likely to be one of the favourites to win the event. Already, Steve was willing to admit that The Swifts was a better choice of name than his own, The Panthers.

There, was, however, one major snag to be overcome: his unavoidable absence in Manchester during the first week of the tournament. Nick hadn't made any comment about that when Steve had mentioned it earlier. He thought he'd better raise the matter again in case Nick hadn't really appreciated the extent of the problem.

'Yeah, it's a bit of a nuisance,' Nick conceded, without sounding unduly perturbed by the situation. For some moments the boys walked on in complete silence. Then Nick halted and faced his companion.

'You'll have to give 'em the slip in Manchester and get back down here in time for the first games,' he declared. 'Then you can stay with us if you like. My mother might not – probably wouldn't – agree to it in advance but she'll take you in if you're homeless. I know her; she falls easily for a good line sometimes. Then, when they know you're safe and with friends, your folks won't try to haul you back to Manchester. I mean, by then they'll be ready to come home themselves, won't they? Well, what do you think of that, Steve?'

Nick's words had taken Steve's breath away. His mind was racing with the impossibility of the idea even as Nick was talking. But at the same time, it was, he recognized, the complete answer to his dilemma. If, that was, he dare attempt it.

'What,' he asked eventually when he felt able to voice his thoughts, 'what do I do if my parents absolutely insist that I go back to Manchester immediately – you know, when I tell them I'm staying with you?'

'Then you go back, don't you?' replied Nick dismissively. 'Point is, by then you'll have played in the first matches and be on your way to winning one of those silver medals. That's the only thing that matters, isn't it?'

'Yeah!' Steve agreed fervently. But he was also thinking of another powerful motive: getting his revenge on Merrywood Colts and The Panthers.

Five

It was a beautiful morning. To Steve, the sight of the sun, shining so early and so brilliantly, was a severe blow. For his purposes, it would have been ideal if Greater Manchester had been drenched by thick mist. Then, once he was out of his grandmother's house, no one would notice him; he'd probably be able to disappear without trace. There'd be no point at all in his parents sending out search parties into the immediate vicinity in the hope of catching sight of him. They'd accept that, in such conditions, it was impossible to locate him.

Steve lowered the corner of the bedroom curtain and started to get dressed. Already he was feeling ravenous even though it wasn't yet six o'clock. But then, he'd been awake for hours; and food was one of the things he'd been thinking about before getting out of bed. Years ago, he'd developed a trick of waking at precisely the time he wanted to:

all he had to do, if he wanted to be up at seven o'clock, was to bang his head seven times on the pillow and keep repeating under his breath 'seven o'clock, seven o'clock' before he fell asleep. However, five o'clock was a target he hadn't tried to hit before and it was probably for that reason he had slept so badly the previous night. Since going to bed he hardly seemed to have slept at all. It was no wonder, he told himself, that he was so hungry. All the same, he was going to keep to his vow not to eat until he was well clear of the house. His pack was already filled with food, hoarded over three days since the weekend, and when he did feel it would be safe to stop for a meal he was going to have a feast. His mouth watered promptly at the thought of it.

He forced himself to think of something else. That wasn't really very difficult because he had a lot to think about. His first task would be the hardest of all: getting hold of his return railway ticket to his home town, Walbridge. When they'd travelled up to Manchester a few days earlier Steve had taken careful note of where his father kept the tickets. They were in a wallet in an inside jacket pocket. There was no reason at all why they shouldn't still be there.

His parents were sleeping in the next room; normally, both of them were heavy sleepers and needed an alarm clock to rise early. On this particular morning they should if anything, be sleeping even more soundly because the previous day they'd taken Steve and his grandmother to Southport. For her benefit, they'd re-visited every one of her favourite haunts in that seaside resort and listened to her constant refrain about how some places had changed out of all recognition and others hadn't altered at all. By the time they'd left the pier, which she'd insisted on saving up for her final treat, they were all near exhaustion. Steve wasn't at all surprised to learn from Gran that it was 'nowadays the longest pier in the whole country'; that's exactly what it felt like. To combat loss of energy he'd eaten everything he'd been offered – and, to his mother's astonishment, asked for more; and, as soon as they were all settled on the train back from Southport to Manchester, he'd fallen asleep. That had been a real bonus. His parents, who hadn't been able to doze because Gran apparently reminisced non-stop throughout the entire journey, had promised themselves a long lie-in the following morning.

With the most delicate touch he opened their door and stepped into the bedroom. His father, a neat and methodical man, had piled his clothes on to a chair and his jacket was draped over the back of it. Steve, after a quick glance at the bed to assure himself that the brilliant morning light hadn't disturbed his parents' sleep, eased the wallet out of

the inside pocket. It took but a moment to remove his own ticket. To his great relief, he didn't fumble a single manœuvre. Moreover, apart from giving an unexpected lurch and uttering a kind of half-suppressed whistle, his father remained unmoved.

Steve, as he went downstairs and avoided the

two creaking steps, began to realize what it must feel like to be a burglar. Still, he told himself, he wasn't taking anything that didn't belong to him (or, more correctly, had not been bought for his exclusive use). He paused outside the room his Gran occupied but all seemed well: there was no sound from within. It was what he expected: although she quite often claimed not to have slept 'a wink all night' his parents grinningly agreed that she was a notorious over-sleeper.

In the kitchen he paused just long enough to leave the note he'd written with such devoted attention to the spelling and the quality of the handwriting. He propped it against the electric toaster, his grandmother's favourite gadget. It read:

> 'Don't worry about me. I'm all right, honest. I've gone back home to play in the Five-a-Side Festival. You know I want to win that medal more than anything. I'm staying with a friend. His mother is very kind and friendly. I'll ring tonight to let you know I've arrived safely.
> Love to all, Steven.'

He hoped the note told them all they needed to know about his absence; he didn't think they would panic and immediately contact the police and railway officials. No doubt his father would quickly discover the disappearance of the ticket: but, by that time, Steve hoped to be halfway to Walbridge. Once he arrived there, they wouldn't know exactly where to look for him. He was glad he'd remembered to add the line about telephoning that evening; they could say what they wanted to then and he would be very polite and listen to every word. With a bit of luck, they'd agree that it was perfectly all right for him to remain with the Abel-Smiths. After all, they could talk to Nick's mother if they wished and hear from her that all was well. Moreover, it would cost his father quite a sum if he had to pay for another rail ticket to and from Manchester.

The amount of traffic on the main road into the city centre surprised him; although he knew that the buses were running he hadn't imagined that quite as many people went to work so early. In the midst of so much activity, there was little likelihood that he would be noticed, he decided comfortingly.

A few moments later he caught sight of the flood-light pylons at Manchester United's ground. Whenever he saw them his imagination soared and he rehearsed the goals he would score at the Stretford End in the crucial FA Cup-tie against Wolverhampton Wanderers. He never could make up his mind whether to complete his hat-trick with a diving header or an unstoppable left-foot drive

('Stevie Sewell demonstrated yet again that he packs a mighty punch in either foot' – *Daily Mirror*) from well outside the penalty area.

So absorbed was he in his thoughts and study of the floodlights that he didn't even notice the police car sliding along the kerb beside him.

'Where are you heading, then, son?' the policeman in the front passenger seat called out to him, startling Steve so much that he tripped over his own feet and almost fell.

'Er – er – home. That's all – just home,' he gasped.

It was unbelievable that the police should have found him so quickly. His parents had been fast asleep – he'd *seen* them – when he left the house only a few minutes ago. How *could* they have alerted the police by this time?

'Where is home, then?' they demanded, giving him no time to work out an alternative. Predict-

ably, up went their eyebrows when they got an answer.

'That's a long way off,' said the driver, a thickset man sporting the kind of moustache worn by Steve's favourite First Division striker. He leaned towards Steve and added: 'Been up to pay homage to the Red Devils' superb amphitheatre, I expect?'

Steven looked so baffled that the second policeman took pity on him. 'He means, my friend does, that he thinks you've been admiring Manchester United's ground. That right?'

'Oh, er, yes,' Steve agreed swiftly. He couldn't think why they didn't just check on his name and then whisk him back to his Gran's house. Surely that was their only purpose in talking to him. He was resigning himself to the complete failure of his mission.

'Thought so,' continued the policeman with a resigned expression on his clean-shaven face. He had very sad-looking dark brown eyes. 'We get thousands – no, it often seems like *millions* – of kids coming up here like you've done, just to gaze admiringly at the wrong bit of Stretford.'

His companion laughed – mockingly, Steve thought. But Steve still hadn't a clue about what was going on. He began to wonder whether they were employing a special new technique designed to get victims to confess to some particular crime without their actually being asked about it.

'Give it up, lad, see the error of your ways,' Brown Eyes was still going on, regardless of Steve's bewilderment. 'Across the road, that's where you ought to be, especially on a summer's day like this one. See a real team, then, wouldn't you?'

'Manchester City?' Steve asked doubtingly.

'Don't be daft! This isn't Moss Side, as well you know. No! Old Trafford – the home of Lancashire C.C.C. To say nothing of being the venue for a few Test Matches. England v. Australia. England v. West Indies. *Real* entertainment, as I keep telling Andy here.'

'Cricket, do you mean?' wondered Steve. He wished he knew what was going on or that they would get to the point of all this crazy questioning; they were just torturing him, going on like this.

'Ever watch any cricket – *Lancashire* cricket?' Andy of the Moustache suddenly asked Steve.

'Er, no, er, not really. You see – '

'EXactly!' The moustache quivered triumphantly. 'It's what I keep telling my old mate here. *Nobody* in his right mind would ever swap even one match of the Reds for a whole *season* over yonder, down Talbot Road, that place called Old Traff-or-summat.'

Before P.c. Sad Eyes could respond to that insult the radio in the car squawked alarmingly. He instantly sat upright, much to Steve's surprise.

From television he was used to policemen acting always in a casual manner, though not the less menacing for that in the right circumstances. Andy was suddenly equally alert.

To Steve, the message being relayed was so garbled that he couldn't grasp more than the occasional word. But he did catch something about 'broken into' and 'still on the premises'. P.c. Andy uttered a clipped reply and switched on his engine.

'Up the Reds!' he shouted to Steve.

And, next moment, the police car had surged away from the kerb, its siren beginning to wail, its roof light flashing excitingly.

Still as bemused as ever by their attitude, Steve, after a final affectionate look at the world famous soccer stadium, hurried on. It never occurred to him that policemen might stop to joke with a schoolboy simply because they were bored on patrol duty and also had some time to kill.

At the bus stop he hadn't long to wait. Shift workers were already there in large numbers. Some of them, after making a comment or two on the subject of the pack he was carrying, said that they wished they had the day off to go fishing – or walking in the country – or just to enjoy themselves doing nothing in particular. They were very envious of Steve's freedom. But then, it really was a lovely day.

Steve thought they were a very friendly lot of

people in Lancashire. Then he remembered that Gran was from Lancashire and he stopped smiling. He began to feel furtive again. Had his parents, he wondered, awakened yet? When the bus came he raced up to the top deck but avoided seats by windows: he wasn't going to risk being spotted from the pavement.

He needn't have worried. The journey to the station was uneventful. There he had only a brief wait before the train he was catching left for Birmingham. Thankfully, no one at all seemed the slightest bit interested in him and he was able to eat a massive breakfast without any interruption; at one point he feared he might be eating far too much, considering the fact that he would soon have to be at his fittest on the football field, but he *was* starving and the more he ate the less he'd have to carry in his pack.

The man at the barrier didn't even glance at him as he punched Steve's ticket and, as he settled in a seat on the opposite side of the carriage from the platform, Steve for the first time since he'd left Gran's house began to feel that he might get to Walbridge without trouble after all.

The soccer magazine he'd brought with him for the journey held his attention only for the first few minutes after the train began to move. He could concentrate on nothing but his thoughts of the Five-a-Side Festival. It was marvellous to know that he was to play for one of the best teams – perhaps *the* best – in the tournament. He didn't think he'd ever be able to thank Nick enough for giving him the chance to join The Swifts; and that made him even more determined not to let Nick down in any way at all. What still amazed Steve was his own courage in taking off like this to achieve a personal ambition; he'd never regarded himself as adventurous and yet here he was in the role of the secret agent outwitting all possible pursuers and about to fulfil a vital mission for his team (er, correction, for his country).

Suddenly, he realized that the woman in the opposite seat was studying him with a rather amused expression.

'Let me guess,' she said, smilingly. 'You're day-dreaming about your summer holiday and the marvellous places you're going to. I'm right, aren't I?'

'Oh no,' Steve replied. 'I'm thinking about the football team I'm playing for. And the Cup we're going to win.'

Her smile swiftly faded. 'Oh, but I thought the football season was over, thank goodness. Doesn't it all end with that big game at Wembley?'

'Definitely not. We're all eager to get going again now.'

She didn't speak to him again for the remainder of the journey. Nor did anyone else. When he changed trains in Birmingham there were so many people about that anyone on the look-out for him might have had great difficulty in spotting him. Even when he stepped on to the platform at Walbridge no one challenged him. He'd made it! He would have liked to punch the air with a goal-scorer's joy but decided he'd better restrain himself.

Then, when he'd crossed the line by the foot-bridge and was leaving the station as casually as he knew how, he discovered that someone was waiting for him after all: Nick Abel-Smith!

The captain of The Swifts was leaning nonchalantly against one of the fluted pillars of the entrance hall. He eased himself away from it as Steve approached but gave no more than a half-smile of welcome.

'Great to see you, Nick!' Steve enthused. 'But I never expected you to come and meet me off the train.'

'Just making sure you'd kept your promise,' Nick said coolly.

'You'd've been in a mess if I hadn't,' remarked Steve cheerfully.

'No, I wouldn't. I've signed up young Rosey Pink from your old team. I thought he showed a bit of promise. And it'll be good for him to get away from Tommy Kent's thugs and into a proper team.'

'Oh,' said Steve, chastened. 'But Pink's not going to take my place, is he?'

'Don't be daft. He hasn't got your speed. And that's what I want. Anyway, let's get off to Higher Wood. I've laid on a secret practice session for us.'

'Secret?'

'Yeah. Tell you about it later. We'll stop for something to eat on the way.'

'Oh, good,' Steve replied, cheering up again. Already, he was feeling famished.

Six

The ball smacked against the trunk of a sapling, rebounded at an oblique angle, struck the exposed root of another tree, shot high in the air: and was killed on his left instep by Nick Abel-Smith. Then, without so much as a half glance to give away his intentions, he flicked the ball sideways into the path of Stevie Sewell.

'Run, Steve, run! Go like mad. Don't stop!'

Steve, for the umpteenth time, did so: sprinting down the narrow corridor between the trees, hoping that he wouldn't trip over hidden obstacles and crash on to his face. He'd suffered that fate once already and the pain still hadn't receded.

Edward Lancaster stepped out from behind a young oak and loomed up in front of him. Steve forced himself not to brake but to swerve past Edward, selling him a dummy with one decisive sway of the hips. Edward went for the ball, crunchingly, and missed it. Gratefully, Steve sped on. But his stamina was ebbing. He knew he couldn't do this another time. This was going to be his last effort.

Lester Rowan crouched. His eyes were on the ball, not on the player racing towards him. The designated goal area in which he stood was rather larger than the normal one but that didn't trouble him. To Lester, keeping goal was all about successfully working out angles: angles from which a player might shoot, angles for narrowing the space at the attacker's disposal. He had studied Steve's play and was aware that he liked to jink one way and slide the ball into the net from the opposite angle. One difficulty in assessing Steve's intentions: he could hit the ball well with either foot.

Neither Nick nor Jazz Fagan had gone up in support. That was Nick's policy in this training session. The front runner had to go solo. Then, if the opposition seized the ball and began a counter-attack, the Swifts' midfielders would be ready to cope with them. The chief striker – Steve, in this instance – had to be prepared to strike without support. That, Nick pointed out, was what the five-a-side game was all about: players having to be confident enough to do things on their own. With only half a team, a member of it could expect at best only half the support he might normally receive.

Steve began to slow up as he came within range of Lester. Unblinkingly, the goalie watched the ball. He remained motionless. In the face of such rigid opposition Steve's concentration wavered. As he edged to his left he looked to his right – and stumbled painfully over a fallen branch. The ball bobbled away, Steve despairingly swung his right foot at it, and as he himself lost his balance the ball soared high into the trees.

It was a moment or two before he thought of getting to his feet. By then the others, with the exception of Nick, had gone to try and retrieve the ball. Nick stood over the fallen striker, hands on hips, his eyes narrowed.

'I just feel whacked, Nick, completely whacked,' Steve confessed.

'You will be whacked – by the opposition – if you make stupid errors like that in a match,' Nick said cuttingly.

'But, Nick, I was thinking about how to score. Worrying about missing from that range. And Lester, well –'

'Look, that's part of your trouble, Steve. You ARE a worrier. Well, I don't want you worrying while you're playing for us. I want you just to run and score goals – by instinct. I'll do all the worrying necessary for all of us. That's my job – as well as showing you how to play, of course. By example.'

Steve gritted his teeth and pushed himself to his feet.

'I've a good reason for being tired, you know,' he pointed out. 'I mean, I was awake half the night and I have travelled hundreds of miles already today.'

'Yeah, O.K. then,' Nick conceded with surprising generosity. 'You have a break and we'll see how young Pink manages in your strike role. I want him to get used to operating in these conditions.'

So Steve stood aside and watched his teammates rehearsing their style of play in the confines of a semi-clearing in Higher Wood. It was, he admitted to himself, a brainwave on Nick's part to think of training in these surroundings where each outfield player had to try and master rough terrain and control the ball when it ricocheted from tree trunks and exposed roots and even low-hanging branches. Nick had explained to them that in five-a-side soccer players rarely had much room to work in and if tight marking were introduced then there were bound to be times when the ball would come at them from unexpected angles. He wanted The Swifts to experience the most difficult conditions possible; then, with a bit of luck, it would be easier for them when they played on a normal pitch in the Festival.

Nick was also determined to keep their tactics as secret as possible – and in Higher Wood they weren't likely to be spotted by any of the other teams. He had decided not to ask other 'spare' players to join them for their training periods, though that meant they could never play a full game as a team. Instead, each of The Swifts had to practise his particular skills against the opposition of his colleagues. But at least, as the skipper had expressed it, they'd never get bored by inactivity! Since arriving in the clearing in mid-afternoon, they hadn't relaxed for a minute.

Although Nick himself was intending to play as co-striker with Steve he was at present concentrating on controlling the midfield in partnership with Jazz Fagan. Here he was able to lay the ball off in a variety of ways for Steve to chase and Jazz to turn into precision-made passes. A player in midfield needed plenty of stamina because he was involved in the action so much; and, despite his apparent frailty in a physical sense, Jazz possessed an abundance of energy. So far, though, Nick hadn't told young Fagan that, if necessary, he might be switched back to a striking role with Nick himself replacing him in the middle of the park. That was a tactical ploy Nick was going to keep up his sleeve for the moment.

Nick wasn't the sort of boy who was always thinking about things in terms of luck (he reckoned you had to work out what you wanted and strive to achieve it, rather than hope for a lucky break). All the same, he recognized that fate must have been on his side when he took a short cut along the line of the old railway and saw Tommy Kent's mob holding a practice session. In addition to finding Steve Sewell, he'd seen that Simon Pink could be a useful player; very likely the boy had much more ability than anyone, including Simon himself, suspected. Certainly he had done the simple things with ease and confidence: and, more important, done them right. Nick had been as impressed as Steve with Simon's reaction to the demand for quick one-twos. It was fairly obvious that Kent would never appreciate Pink's budding talent and so wouldn't make use of him in his team in a constructive way.

Simon had been just as flattered as Steve to receive an approach from Nick Abel-Smith and accordingly had agreed without hesitation to join his squad. As he wasn't exactly brimming over with arrogance he was perfectly content with the promise that he'd not be kept as permanent substitute but would get into the team at some stage.

Now, having taken Steve's place as chief striker in the woodland training spell, Simon was demonstrating splendid qualities of pace and perseverance. Nick, who had been feeding him some deliberately awkward passes, was thoroughly impressed. Steve was looking increasingly worried. One of their team-mates, Edward Lancaster, was becoming a bit fed-up with this particular routine. After all, he was the one who had to do all the really hard work of tackling and intercepting as the only 'stopper' in the side. Unlike Jazz, he hadn't a partner to help him out. All too often, Edward was also suffering the worst of the effects of the ground conditions: the unpredictable bounce of the ball meant that he had to do a lot of sharp turns and twists, whereas his opponent kept going forward all the time.

Twice Simon slipped easily past the solidly-built, red-haired defender and each time, as a result of his smart footwork, he managed to put the ball into the back of the imaginary net. The third time he appeared to be on the verge of repeating that feat Edward felled him with a really crushing tackle that would have earned him, in a competitive game, a yellow card and a severe talking to from the referee. Nick took it as a sign to bring the training session to an end. On the eve of their first match in the Festival nothing would be worse for the team's morale than for individuals to start building up a sense of resentment against one another for *any* reason.

'O.K., lads, let's pack it in for today,' he told them cheerfully. 'You've all worked terrifically hard and I'm pleased with the way things have gone. If we play in the Festival as I know now we can play then we'll win it. No doubt about that. We'll win it for ourselves and we'll win it for our sponsors. And don't forget: the medals will last a lifetime.'

He paused significantly after uttering that carefully worked out phrase. He saw that it had an immediate effect on his team – his half-team, as he thought of it. Every one of them wanted to win that Cup and the medals just as much as he did. That was the way it should be.

'Right, then. We'll all assemble at my house at 10.30 in the morning for a final tactical talk. Get a good night's sleep and don't worry about anything. The opposition will be the ones doing the worrying.'

Steve, walking home with Nick, wondered whether any of the others had even *half* as much to worry them as he had. For he still had no idea whether his parents would allow him to remain at Nick's home tonight and for the remainder of the week. Much would depend on how successfully he presented his case when he telephoned them.

He was comforted, though, by the welcome he'd received from Mrs Abel-Smith. She said her intention was to make him feel 'completely at home' and the lunch she provided was at least as good as his own mother could provide (Nick, however, had warned him not to eat too much and so Steve had dutifully and politely refused second helpings). What Steve didn't quite realize was that Shirley Abel-Smith was as delighted to have him stay with them as he was to be there. She had begun to despair of her only son's ever having a really close friend; Nick, of course, spent a lot of time with other boys just by playing football but he built no lasting friendships with any of them. Quite the reverse, in fact: almost as soon as he got to know another boy well, he fell out with him. So far as Mrs Abel-Smith could judge, the cause of the upset between Nick and others was always to do with football and the failure of the other players to grasp what Nick expected of them. Nick could be really scathing about their lack of ability. But, apart from his comments on that subject, her son said remarkably little about his activities outside the home.

Steve was the first boy he'd ever invited to stay overnight and Mrs Abel-Smith took it as a sign that, at last, Nick had found someone whose company he thoroughly enjoyed. So she was determined that Steve shouldn't suffer a moment's unhappiness while he was their guest; everything that could be done to ensure that he wasn't home-sick for a single moment *would* be done. She moved the spare bed into Nick's room so that the pals (as she described them to her husband and neighbours) could be together all the time. Nick himself wasn't too charmed by the idea and told Steve when they were on their own: 'I hope you don't yell out or make loud noises in the middle of the night. I need a full night's sleep before a vital match.' Steve said he kept as silent as the grave and hoped that was true.

So, after their evening meal, it was Mrs Abel-Smith who telephoned Manchester and talked soothingly and at length to Steve's parents. She was as charming as her son could be off-hand or abusive and managed eventually to convince Mr and Mrs Sewell that by showing such enterprise, Steve deserved to play in the Festival matches. When Mr Sewell actually confessed to her that he and his wife felt they'd been a little unfair in taking Steve with them just when he'd set his heart on taking part in the tournament, Mrs Abel-Smith winked at Steve.

At that moment, Steve knew everything was going to be all right after all. His personal worries were over: now he could concentrate wholly on giving the best football performance of his life.

Seven

Their shirts were black and white and though the colours couldn't match the plumage of a swift they were the best that could be obtained at short notice. In any case, the boys who were wearing them were simply happy to have an outfit that had been provided solely for their use: and which, moreover, they could keep when the Festival was over. Not for the first time since they'd come together under his leadership, The Swifts told each other how much they admired Nick's organizing ability and his unrelenting determination to get what he wanted. For it was he, entirely on his own initiative, who had found a sponsor for the team.

Nick was well aware that any squad's morale could be boosted by the promise of fashionable new kit to be worn for special matches; and he wanted his players to feel good and look good when they went on to the pitch for their first Cup-tie. He couldn't expect them to pay for shirts, shorts and socks at a moment's notice but it hadn't taken him long to think of approaching a local business firm and asking them for the necessary money. In return for their sponsorship the firm would be mentioned in the official programme for the Festival and perhaps secure further publicity in the evening newspaper's reports of the matches involving The Swifts.

However, it was Jazz Fagan who had the idea of contacting a company that imported and sold motor-cycles. Rather to Nick's surprise, Jazz turned out to be a motocross fanatic and had every intention one day of competing as a rider himself. It seemed that whenever he was in the town centre he spent at least several minutes gazing admiringly at the gleaming bikes in the firm's showroom.

When Nick had casually mentioned that he was off to town in search of a suitable sponsor Jazz had recommended trying the motor-cycle company. 'They believe in speed, don't they? So they ought to support us Swifts. Oh, and their general manager is a soccer fan. I know because we often have a chat about football when he sees me looking in his window.'

Gaining the firm's support had been much easier than Nick had expected: they appeared delighted to help out and had promised a bonus ('not cash but something I'm sure you'll all enjoy') if the Swifts reached the final of the tournament. With the money the firm supplied for kit and one or two other expenses Nick had been able to put something aside for any emergency that might crop up; it was out of his own pocket, though, that he

paid for various titbits his cousin, Ann-Marie, gave to Atkins, Lester Rowan's Irish Setter. It was in another moment of inspiration that Nick had remembered that Ann-Marie was as crazy about animals as Lester was; so she had needed no persuading at all to look after Atkins in Lester's absence.

When the team assembled at Nick's house on the morning that the Festival was launched Lester was the last to turn up. He was almost out of breath and looked distinctly troubled by something.

'What's up?' Nick asked him anxiously. Lester was indispensable. They had no one else who could take over in goal. 'Is Atkins all right?'

'Oh, er, Atkins is fine – everything's fine,' Lester replied, suddenly grinning. 'I just got held up on the way here, that's all. Nothing at all to worry about, Nick.'

'Good,' replied Nick, not altogether convinced that all was well. But there was no time now to make further inquiries. In a few minutes they'd have to leave for Lowbell Lane where the matches were being played. So this was their last chance for him to impress upon his players the need to play at all times the way they'd rehearsed throughout their training sessions.

'Don't forget that Shapton Wanderers are a very experienced side and they, too, may play it very cool to start with,' he reminded them. 'But we mustn't be tempted to speed things up just for the sake of a bit of action. We're going to play this match *our* way. Don't let any of the spectators put you off, either. They're bound to yell stupid things at the players. But just ignore 'em!'

As it turned out, that wasn't going to be easy. For the crowd that had already arrived at the sports ground for the first matches was much bigger than any of the players had expected. Five pitches were being used, each one very neatly roped-off so that spectators didn't encroach on the playing areas. Overall, there was something of a fairground atmosphere with stalls selling soft drinks and refreshments, along with those offering prizes for guessing the number of small coins in a goldfish bowl or lobbing table tennis balls into narrow-necked jars. Raffle tickets were being distributed enthusiastically among the strollers and a centre of attention was a mobile badge factory. For only a few pence individuals, or teams, could order, in a variety of colours and complete with slogan, their own metal, pin-on badge; as soon as the artwork was completed the badge would be manufactured almost instantaneously on the spot by the salesman-cum-machine-operator. As the word spread, and the finished badges were displayed by their wearers, he was almost overwhelmed by further orders.

'They're for the teams that haven't got anything

else to shout about,' scoffed Nick. 'We'll *prove* we're the best by winning. Nobody can argue with cups and medals.'

Edward Lancaster, for one, looked disappointed that The Swifts weren't going to display badges but he'd never opposed Nick in anything since they'd been on the same side and he wasn't going to start now. For the umpteenth time since it had been made public, Nick was studying the draw for the first round matches; this particular sheet was pinned to a stretch of fencing beside the ice-cream van. Edward strolled across to join Nick and listen to the predictable comments about the likely outcome of the various pairings.

The draw hadn't really pleased any member of Nick's team. The Swifts couldn't meet until the later stages of the competition any of the opponents they most wanted to thrash: Oakland Rangers, Bank Vale United (a team both Edward and Nick had played for), Tommy Kent's Panthers or Merrywood Colts, the side that had originally rejected Steve Sewell. Then, in the first round, they'd been matched with a Sunday League side, Shapton Wanderers, which had played extremely well in the final weeks of the League season and only just missed Championship honours. Nick's confidence, though, hadn't waned: Wanderers, he pointed out with a nice turn of phrase picked up from a soccer magazine, would help to put a cutting edge on The Swifts' attack. None of the defenders had the temerity to ask Nick what effect Wanderers' play was going to have on them.

When, at last, The Swifts were summoned to Pitch No. 3 to start their game they suffered an early shock. Unaccountably, Lester Rowan fumbled a first-time shot from Wanderers' bustling striker – and the ball trickled over the line into the net. That was after only twenty-three seconds of the match.

Nick stared disbelievingly, Lester's expression flickered between embarrassment and horror, Edward Lancaster swallowed hard and succeeded in saying nothing: and, when the cheers of Wanderers' supporters died away, someone behind Lester's net jeered: 'That was rubbish, Goalie, sheer rubbish! Pity we're not playing your side.' The voice was that of Tommy Kent; and, as if on cue, his fellow Panthers started to guffaw.

'Sorry, Nick, don't know what I was thinking about,' Lester muttered when his captain came within earshot. That was not strictly true: Lester knew exactly why he'd been so distracted. But he daren't admit the reason to Nick Abel-Smith of all people.

'If that's the best you can do, stop thinking altogether,' said Nick caustically. 'You couldn't do worse with an empty head!'

The goal had been scored by Ian Penn, the one

really dangerous player in Shapton's team according to Nick. Penn was exceptionally strong on the ball with a facility for riding even the toughest tackles; and his shooting skills had disarmed many goalkeepers. Nonetheless, a player of Rowan's class should have stopped that particular shot without any difficulty at all. For Nick, the match couldn't have started in more worrying fashion: his goalkeeper was fallible and the opposition's leading scorer had just had his confidence boosted astronomically.

'Don't let him get away from you again,' Nick told Edward threateningly, with a nod in Ian Penn's direction. 'Fix him!'

Five-a-side was hardly a game for man-to-man marking when you were a goal down but Nick felt he had no option but to switch to that tactic for the moment. His team had to have time to settle down. It would be utterly disastrous if they conceded another goal in the next two or three minutes.

With Edward harnessing Ian Penn and Nick remaining in midfield, just as he'd planned to do, the game was soon viewed as a bore by many spectators. They drifted away to find real entertainment elsewhere. Up-field, Steve Sewell was almost equally bored by the proceedings. He hadn't managed a single kick yet; indeed the ball hadn't been within metres of him since the kick-off. He cautiously moved back towards the middle until Nick spotted what he was up to and imperiously waved him back.

Then, as if tiring of such limiting play, Jazz Fagan took it into his head to go on a solo run. The move took his team-mates as well as the Wanderers by surprise and, for the first time since the game began, Shapton's goalkeeper actually handled the ball. Jazz shot on the run when within sight of goal and the goalie almost turned it aside for a corner. It was just as well for his side that he didn't; a corner earned the attacking side one point and points might decide the result of a match if, at the end of normal playing time, the scores were level.

Instinctively, Steve had raced through to give support. His speed off the mark plainly took the Shapton defenders by surprise. Although the ball never reached him, Steve had already done enough to sow alarm among the opposition.

Jazz, thrilled to have made some positive contribution at last, began to push the ball around with increasing confidence, looking for an opportunity to create a breakaway for Steve or Nick. In his present mood, the skipper wasn't keen on all-out attacking. On the other hand, with only five minutes' play in each half, he couldn't restrict The Swifts' strategy to containment indefinitely. Apart from that initial lapse, his defenders were playing solidly and Ian Penn was being given no chance to

add to his score. Edward looked to be glued to the Wanderers' striker.

Penn, however, was a resourceful player. He was used to having defenders try to put a stranglehold on him. So he'd developed a few tricks to deal with that situation. As soon as he was about to be involved in a tussle for the ball he backed into his marker; and then, immediately, catapulted forward as if he'd been charged in the back. It was a dodge that frequently won him a free kick for foul play: and it succeeded again now in spite of Edward's outraged claims to be innocent. The referee told the Swifts defender to shut up or suffer the consequences. Edward shut up.

Ian Penn took the kick himself, blasting the ball towards the bottom right-hand corner of the net. He had done well in keeping the shot low but not well enough to beat Lester who scooped the ball up nonchalantly with both hands and, in the same movement, rolled it out to Jazz to ferry it upfield.

Half-a-minute later, and almost on the stroke of half-time, Penn put in another bit of sharp practice to earn his team a second free kick. This time, as Edward very neatly brought the ball under control, Penn collapsed in a heap, dramatically clutching the back of his ankle. From that position he still managed to convey the impression that it was only because he was exercising the greatest self-discipline that he wasn't yelling with agony.

'One more foul like that and you're out of this competition for good, I'll see to that!' the referee said fiercely to Edward while showing him a yellow card for an official caution. 'You could ruin a player for life, kicking him on the ankle like that.'

Edward had the sense to realize that the referee, who was all too obviously biased, wouldn't listen to a word of his defence against that charge. Shrugging his shoulders and raising his eyes to the heavens, he walked away. Shapton's trainer/manager/physiotherapist, who also happened to be Ian Penn's father, dashed on to the pitch, firing furious glances at the alleged offender.

This time, with young Penn still writhing on the ground it had to be another player to take the free kick. The distance was shorter, the chance of scoring greater: but, once again, Lester fielded the ball with supreme competence and Shapton's hopes of doubling their lead had gone.

As soon as the referee brought the first half to an end the players went into huddles around their respective captains. Simon Pink came on to the field with a bag of oranges that had already been cut into halves so that no time would be wasted before enjoying them. Nick's planning could not be faulted in any aspect of the game.

His players rather expected to be berated, if only for losing that early goal. Instead, Nick was calm and reassuring.

'It's going well. We're doing all right. Shapton have had their chances and missed 'em. They're panicking – that's why that idiot Penn is trying to get Edward here sent off. They know we're bound to attack 'em in the second half. Dead right. We will.'

Lester Rowan nodded approvingly. It would be a nice change to see the other goalmouth under siege. He knew that Wanderers' goalie wasn't very reliable under pressure; his reputation, such as it was, had been built on his general athleticism and talent for bringing off the occasional world-beating save.

It was Ian Penn, looking perfectly fit again and, if possible, even more aggressive than usual, who kicked off for the second half. Rather to his surprise, Edward homed in on him again without delay. This time, Edward's presence rattled him.

'Don't forget, you'll get sent off if you touch me again,' he muttered. Edward's only response was to grin and say nothing. Then, when the ball came their way, it was Edward who moved the faster to collect it.

Instead of following his usual custom of transferring the ball to Jazz or Nick, Edward this time accelerated along the touch-line. His strength enabled him to repel two fierce attempts to dispossess him. Then, after checking that Steve was as free as he'd expected him to be, he yelled 'Stevie!' and in the same instant fired the ball to a point well ahead of his team-mate.

That ploy was just about the last Shapton seemed to expect. Their defenders had spent so much time upfield they'd almost forgotten their original role. But, even if they hadn't hesitated before pursuing him, Steve Sewell would still have outrun them easily. The pass from Edward was as good as any he could have received from Nick or

Jazz and he wasn't going to waste it after waiting so long for his chance.

Despairingly, the exposed goalkeeper advanced to the limit of his half-circle. That was exactly what Steve hoped he'd do. Without breaking his stride, The Swifts' striker turned fractionally to his left to pull the goalie still further in that direction; and then with his left foot he drove the ball firmly past him into the far corner of the net. The ball kept so low it would have decapitated any daisies on its path: the shot couldn't have been struck any better.

Nick looked on approvingly as the rest of their team-mates showered Steve with congratulations. Everything was going according to his plan; and, just as he'd expected, Shapton Wanderers went furiously on to the attack when the game re-started. But, once again, The Swifts' strength in midfield kept them at bay. Ian Penn tried every ruse he knew to provoke Edward into committing a foul: but Edward refused to be drawn. In any case, he was thoroughly enjoying the way he was playing.

Less than a minute of normal playing time remained when, deflected by Penn's ankle, the ball went out of play on The Swifts' left flank. Edward promptly rolled the ball back to Nick who, giving a pre-arranged signal by raising his right arm vertically, switched the ball to Jazz. In turn, Jazz flicked it back to Edward, now progressing smartly down the left wing.

The passes were interchanged with such rapidity and precision that the Wanderers hadn't a hope of an interception. No one was more bewildered than the goalkeeper. He had no idea at all where the final shot would come from – left, centre or right. In fact, it was made by Steve, right-footed this time but as powerful and accurate as his first shot. The end result was the same and the goal was applauded by every single spectator. Unfortunately, they numbered only twenty-six; up to that point the match hadn't been very stimulating for casual observers.

Nick was completely satisfied with the narrowness of The Swifts' victory in the first round of the Festival.

'Just what we wanted. No publicity, no excitement. The story'll get around that we played defensive football to win. Some people'll think it was a fluke we won at all. O.K., let 'em. If other teams think we're a pushover that suits us fine. We'll just creep away with the Cup if we have to – if that's the way to win it. Anyway, let's go and see some of the other sides in action. Give ourselves a chance of assessing the opposition we might meet.'

As it happened, they were just in time to see The Panthers playing a very useful side called Clayton's Villa. The Villa were led by a boy called Frankie Clayton, the actual founder of the team and the son of a rich and keen supporter of Aston Villa. Frankie himself played centre-forward, very much in the style of Ian Penn.

It was, as Nick pointed out, completely predictable that Frankie Clayton and Tommy Kent, directly opposing each other as striker and central defender, should clash physically as well as emotionally: and that Tommy, after two stern warnings from the referee, should be sent off for misconduct.

Thereafter The Panthers quickly disintegrated and were swept out of the tournament. After the way his old team-mates had treated him, Steve couldn't feel much sympathy for them. Later he saw another of his former teams, Merrywood Colts, win one match comfortably but lose the next, to Bank Vale United.

The following day, when the second series of matches was played, it was Nick's turn to see the defeat of one of his old teams: Oakland Rangers were comprehensively outplayed by Clayton's Villa. But then, very surprisingly, Villa themselves played poorly against their next opponents and were knocked out of the competition.

With no change at all in their playing strategy – frustrating the opposition in midfield and scoring usually only on breakaways – The Swifts continued to progress, winning each game by a narrow margin. Even in the semi-final they defended for ninety-five per cent of the time and then gained their victory through a well-organized free kick in the last minute. The cheers from the crowd when they came off the field were unarguably lukewarm.

'Who cares about what those fans think?' was Nick's reaction to the lack of appreciation for his team's achievement. 'I bet they'll still turn up to see us play in the Final. And then they'll get a surprise or two.'

He was right about that, too.

Eight

Spectacular was the only way to describe the arrival of Nick Abel-Smith and The Swifts on Finals Day at Lowbell Lane Sports Ground. True to their promise, the team's sponsor had arranged something out of the ordinary: each player was taken from the town centre on the back of a brand-new, high-powered motor-cycle. The cavalcade then made a circuit of the pitches with the boys, already dressed in their black-and-white soccer gear, each clutching a polka-dot football in one hand and waving to the assembled spectators with the other. The photographers had a busy time and, although five Finals were being played in the various age-groups that day, it was the picture of The Swifts on motor-bikes that caught the eye on the sports page of the next issue of the local paper.

'I suppose,' somebody remarked, 'this is the modern version of The Entry of the Gladiators!'

The motor-cycle riders lined up their machines a few metres from the pitch after the footballers had dismounted; within seconds they were surrounded by enthusiasts who hoped they might be invited to have a free ride before the tournament was over.

Nick was quite delighted with the effect their arrival had had on so many of the people present. But one person in particular was not impressed in the slightest degree.

'You'll need more than gimmicks to beat us, Smithy,' remarked Keith Nash, captain of Bank Vale United, The Swifts' opponents in the Final. 'Goals are the only thing that count in the match

and you haven't been scoring any lately. You won't get any today, either.'

'Just shows how little you know!' Nick retaliated. 'Any five-a-side match can be won with just one *point* for getting a corner. But don't worry, *skipper*. We'll knock a few goals in as well to emphasize our superiority.'

In a previous season both Nick and Edward Lancaster had played for Bank Vale and thus knew three of their players very well: Nash, the fair-haired midfielder; Kevin Ripley, the effervescent striker who had once been so pally with Nick he'd described him as a genius on a football field; and Gary Ansell, the speedy right-winger. The other two players were newcomers to the present United side.

For once the normally boastful Ripley seemed subdued. He didn't speak a word to Nick as the teams lined up on the pitch after being presented to the Mayor from whom, in less than twenty minutes, winners and runners-up would receive their medals. As it was a final they were to play seven minutes each way with an interval of two minutes. Rather in the style of the man in charge of a boxing match, the referee had already told both captains that he wanted 'a clean game – no dirty tricks, no sly fouling by anybody. Remember, a lot of these spectators normally see only professional football with all its horrors. So let's show them that the youngsters of today play the game in a decent, *sporting* way.'

Inevitably, the first attack was launched by Bank Vale but it carried little conviction and therefore posed no threat to The Swifts' by now thoroughly well organized defence. Jazz Fagan had been deputed to look after Ripley and he was quick to demonstrate to the United player that he possessed a biting tackle as well as great control of the ball in tight situations. Nick grinned at the thought that it had been a masterstroke to convert a front-runner into a tigerish midfield player: and, what's more, Jazz's real pace was still in reserve. That speed would be employed when it was really needed.

For the moment, however, both sides were playing only tentatively. Irritated by this lack of real action one loud-voiced spectator yelled: 'Come on you lot, get stuck in! Give us something worth watching!'

Hardly were the words out of his mouth than a dog raced across the pitch like a streak of red lightning. United were trying to attack again at that point and, in its headlong rush to the goalmouth, the dog bundled the ball away from the foot of Kevin Ripley. Then, with a joyous leap, the dog hurled itself into the arms of Lester Rowan. Naturally: it was, of course, his dog. Hastily, he pushed it away from him.

'Atkins!' he thundered, overcoming his surprise with commendable speed. 'Sit!'

And, quite instantaneously, Atkins sat – and awaited the next word of command. He was reunited with his master and that was what mattered to him.

'Best thing that's happened so far,' called the vocal spectator. 'Nice line in training dumb animals you lads have got. Keep it up!'

The referee was one person on the ground who wasn't amused by Atkins' antics. Having established that Lester was the owner he reprimanded the goalie for being so foolish as to take a dog to a football match. As he did so, however, Ann-Marie stepped bashfully forward to explain that she was officially in charge of the animal but in its eagerness to see its master it had pulled itself free of her. Nick, who hadn't said a word so far, noted the looks his cousin and Lester exchanged. It had never occurred to him that Lester and Ann-Marie might become so fond of each other they didn't want to be apart if there was a chance to be together. He guessed now why Lester had been so abstracted during their first round match – doubtless he was checking whether his girl friend had turned up!

Still, on this occasion Atkins' presence hadn't done The Swifts any harm. United might have deserved a free kick for the way the Red Setter tackled Ripley but the referee decided play should re-start with a dropped ball. Jazz neatly hooked it away from Ripley's ankles and sent Edward away with a good pass.

'I suppose that rotten dog's your secret weapon, Smithy!' Kevin Ripley snarled.

Nick smiled cheerfully and replied: 'Woof, woof!'

A few moments later Ripley, at last breaking away from Jazz's stranglehold, managed to get in a tremendous shot that he was sure would bring United their first goal. Instead, Lester Rowan knocked it up and then caught it against his chest, almost in the manner of a slip fielder at cricket, as it came down. Plainly, Lester was in his old superlative form.

With half-time only seconds away the ball went out of play close to the half-way line. It was Nick who grabbed the ball: and, as he did so, he tapped his right knee. Edward, standing just inside United's half, saw the signal and knew that the ball would be rolled all the way back to him. It was. Edward, hitting his shot with all the power he possessed, had a clear sight of goal – and the ball flashed into the top of the net. It was the first time The Swifts had worked that trick and it succeeded perfectly.

Edward flung his arms into the air and then jumped high with glee. Not only had he scored his first goal of the tournament, he'd scored it against his former team-mates. The pace and accuracy of the shot left the United players looking dumbfounded. What's more, before they had time to stir themselves into action the referee blew for half-time. For Bank Vale, the blow had fallen at the worst psychological moment.

For The Swifts, there was cause for a double celebration: Edward's first goal had provided them with their first ever lead at half-time. 'I reckon Ann-Marie's brought us luck,' grinned Lester as Nick's cousin, along with Atkins, joined them. 'She wanted to come to earlier matches but I wouldn't let her – not after the first one, anyway. I was dead scared Atkins would pull her arms off and get free!'

'We don't need luck, we're doing well enough

without it,' said Nick, adding with unusual gallantry, 'though we're all glad to see you, Ann-Marie. I think Atkins had better be our mascot from now on. Then if the defence is in trouble we can release him to upset the opposition!'

The Swifts' mood was so obviously relaxed that neutral spectators had no doubt at all that the team in black-and-white would win easily. Bank Vale United looked so completely depressed. With Kevin Ripley out of form and shackled by Jazz Fagan their attack wasn't functioning at all.

Nick, who was aware of that situation, decided that The Swifts should go on the offensive from the moment the second-half began. No one was happier than he to abandon defensive play and, with Stevie giving him close support, he turned on some exhilarating displays of ball control and precision passing. Having played against him in the League and in training session, he knew perfectly how to outwit Keith Nash, a solid but uninspired midfield player.

Within a minute of the re-start it was Nick himself who put the ball in the net, deftly side-stepping Nash's challenge and then sweeping home a pass from Steve. Fifty seconds later Nick scored again with a dipping volley when United's goalie was well off his line.

Soon after that The Swifts' captain, as if satisfied with his own contribution to the score-line, took up a midfield position again. Although realizing that they had no hope of winning now, United were still staging the occasional attack, only to founder if they got as far as Lester Rowan's zone.

It was while United were attempting to drive forward that Nick coolly intercepted a pass and, spotting an opening, supplied Jazz with the perfect pass and the injunction: 'Go!'

Jazz went, at astonishing speed, all on his own and with only the goalie to beat: and he beat the demoralized goalkeeper with ease. He was as overjoyed as Edward had been at scoring his first goal of the Five-a-Side Festival. It was also the final goal of the Final. The Swifts 4, Bank Vale United 0.

Disappointed though he was with the outcome, Keith Nash had a word for his old team-mate, Nick Abel-Smith. 'Well done. I've got to admit it – you were brilliant today. I just wish you were still playing for us.'

Nick smiled, slapped Keith on the back and went to collect the trophy. As the players waited for the Mayor to make the presentations Nick turned to the team mate standing behind him.

'Sorry you didn't get a goal today – but your goals got us through the early rounds, remember.'

'Oh, I don't care about not scoring today,' replied Steve Sewell with a huge grin. 'We won the Cup – and I get a medal. That's what really counts, isn't it?'